Captain John Smith and His Critics

Also from Westphalia Press
westphaliapress.org

Captain John Smith and His Critics

by Charles Poindexter

WESTPHALIA PRESS
An imprint of Policy Studies Organization

Westphalia Press
An imprint of Policy Studies Organization
1527 New Hampshire Ave., NW
Washington, D.C. 20036
info@ipsonet.org

ISBN-13: 978-1-63391-239-7
ISBN-10: 1633912396

Cover design by Taillefer Long at Illuminated Stories:
www.illuminatedstories.com

Daniel Gutierrez-Sandoval, Executive Director
PSO and Westphalia Press

Updated material and comments on this edition
can be found at the Westphalia Press website:
www.westphaliapress.org

Captain JOHN SMITH

AND HIS CRITICS.

A Lecture before the Society for

GEOGRAPHICAL AND HISTORICAL STUDY

of Richmond College,

BY

CHARLES POINDEXTER,

Acting Librarian of the Virginia State Library.

RICHMOND.

1893.

To

The Society for Geographical and Historical Study

of Richmond College,

before whom this Lecture was delivered,

and by whose request it

is printed.

"Those old credulities, to nature dear,
  Shall they no longer bloom upon the stock
  Of history, stript naked as a rock
  'Mid a dry desert ? . . . . .
          If Truth, who veiled her face
  With those bright beams yet hid it not, must steer
  Henceforth a humbler course, perplexed and slow ;
  One solace yet remains for us who came
  Into this world in days when story lacked
  Severe research, that in our hearts we know
  How, for exciting youth's heroic flame,
  Assent is power, belief the soul of fact."

CAPTAIN JOHN SMITH

AND HIS CRITICS.

" Fellow, either thou art the cunningest liar that ever earned a halter, or else thou hast done a deed the like of which never man ventured."—*Charles Kingsley.*

It is a trite comment, often verified, that the results of an historical crisis generally disappoint the predictions as to its probable hero, who will stamp on its history the indelible impress of his personality, linking his name and fame with its memory. Seldom has this comment been more signally illustrated than in the history of the man and events to which we propose some consideration; for, when Capt. John Smith sailed from England with his fellow-colonists, he was distinguished by very little of the fame which now makes him illustrious, and when they arrived in Virginia John Smith was actually under arrest, and in such disfavor with some of his comrades that he was denied his rightful rank and position as a member of the Council; which denial was the result of differences and feuds during the long and perilous voyage across the Atlantic.

It looks like the irony of fate, that of that band of Englishmen, men of all sorts, who entered our capes on that April day of 1607, and then proceeded to organize under instructions of the company who sent them over—of all that band of men the name of John Smith, then in such disgrace as rivalry or enmity could put upon him, is yet to-day the one name known and remembered; the others forgotten or unknown, except to those curious in historic details, and recalled or referred to mainly, or only, to illustrate Smith's history.

A most striking fact to be noted is this immense force of Smith's strength of character and his personality, which has so projected itself over our early history that the common idea seems to credit him with planning the colony, bringing it over, and settling it. As a matter of fact, he was only one of a number of volunteers sent over by a trading colonial company, was in Virginia only about two and a half years, and became governor (so called) only in the last months of his stay.

But how his name and fame did and does survive! with such living force that his deeds and character are discussed to-day, when he is dead two hundred and fifty years, with a zeal and energy not often evoked for a living personage.

The limits of this occasion forbid any elaborate introduction of the subject, and allow but brief and scant notice of Smith's early history, or of the character and spirit of the age in which he lived and acted his part—knowledge and note of which latter is essentially necessary for any proper understanding of him and his life. Lacking time for the setting of this historic back-ground, I can only refer you to histories of the period and to the numerous works on and studies of that age in which our recent literature is particularly rich.

In Charles Kingsley's "Westward, Ho!" that great romance of war and adventure, whose scenes are laid in England just before John Smith's time, you may remember that marvellous narrative of Salvation Yeo's adventures on the Spanish Main, which he recounts while subjected to examination by Sir Richard Grenville and Amyas Leigh; you may remember that, on reaching the climax of his story, he is interrupted by Sir

Richard's exclamation: "Fellow, either thou art the cunningest liar that ever earned a halter, or else thou hast done a deed the like of which never man ventured." You may remember, further, that being checked all along by reference to facts well known to his hearers, Salvation Yeo vindicates his character and truthfulness before the stern questioning of so rugged a critic as Sir Richard Grenville.

Your attention is invited to some facts and considerations bearing on charges made affecting the veracity and character of the hero of an adventure in real life—the most romantic in American annals—and from these facts we shall try to prove that the father of Virginia history, in both the actual and literary sense, the hero and chronicler of this adventure, was not a liar, cunning or uncunning.

It was an age of great and, when occasion called for them, of daring deeds, in which John Smith was born and lived his life as depicted in his works and known to us; a life, the natural product of his age and char- acteristic of the temper and thoughts of thousands of men of his time—

"The spacious times of great Elizabeth,"

as the poet of our day calls them. How spacious and how great, we learn better to understand as we know more of the character and deeds of the men who made the age renowned. It was an age of great thoughts and of great men, some of whom have stamped the impress of their genius on the world for all time; an age of great enterprises and beginnings of yet greater ones, whose developement has made English and American history of the last three centuries, and changed the destiny and aspects of the whole world.

Among the heroes of that age John Smith has been deemed not unworthy of an honorable fame—a distinction generally conceded to him by his contemporaries and by succeeding generations, but questioned and denied by the criticism and opinion of some in these later modern days. Denied by CRITICISM and OPINION, we say; for the adverse judgment that denounces John Smith as a lying braggart cannot be said to be founded on any discovery of new facts unknown to previous generations, but is an assumption based on statements attributed to Smith himself, as to matters of fact that have long been accepted as familiar truths of history.

For any proper understanding of him and

the questions involved, a brief statement of the leading facts of Smith's life is necessary, premising, as always essential, a reference to the character and spirit of his time as a background to the picture of his life and exploits.

Perhaps the character of the age is best indicated in brief by noting that when Smith was born, Queen Elizabeth was forty-six years old, Sir Walter Raleigh twenty-seven, Lord Bacon eighteen, Shakspeare fifteen, and Ben Jonson five years old; and that when Howard, Drake, and Hawkins fought and beat the Spanish armada, John Smith was a boy of nine years.

In this England of Elizabeth, in the year 1579, John Smith was born of honest, plain parents, who probably made an excellent living on their Lincolnshire farm. His father was a yeoman farmer, able to give his children such education as the neighborhood schools afforded, and to leave them some property at his death, which occurred when John was thirteen years old. About all we know of his early years is summed up in the introductory paragraphs of his own account of himself, in which he tells us that he was "scholar in the two free schools of Louth" "and Alford. His parents dying when he"

" was about thirteen, left him a competent "
" means, which he, not being capable to "
" manage, little regarded. His mind even "
" then being set upon brave adventures, he "
" sold his satchel and books and all he had,"
" intending secretly to get to sea, but that "
" his father's death stayed him. About the "
" age of fifteen he was bound apprentice to "
" the greatest merchant in all those parts, "
" but because he would not presently send "
" him to sea he never saw his master in "
" eight years after." In other words, he
took his fate in his own hands and started
off on a course of adventure in France and
the Low countries, where he spent the next
four or five years learning his business of
soldiering. From the same chapter of his
memoirs, here is a picture of himself on a
visit, after this long absence, to his old home
at Willoughby: "Where, after a short time, "
" being glutted with too much company, "
" wherein he took small delight, he retired "
" himself into a little woody pasture, a "
" good way from any town. Here by a fair "
" brook he built himself a pavilion of "
" boughs, where only in his clothes he lay. "
" His STUDY was Machiavelli's Art of War "
" and Marcus Aurelius; his exercise a "
" good horse with his lance and ring."

Here was an adventurer quite different from the common run of them, whose leisure i generally given to fast living and hard drinking. Fancy him, if you can, this youth of twenty, in his Arden-like retreat, studying Machiavelli and Marcus Aurelius; and this no dilettant, mere literary perusal of those classics, but the serious study of a manly youth with four years of rough soldiering behind him to illustrate and improve the wisdom of the lessons learned from those great masters, whose teachings stood him well in after years, informing and training his natural sense, and helping to develope qualities that made him a born leader of men. Pity that they did not also improve his literary style, which is rough to a degree that makes him hard reading till we find under it the masterly sense and charm of a real man. However, he was not training for scholarship, and his thoughts were probably not much about the graces of literature. Quite otherwise, as he proved, when at first chance he betook himself again to campaigning, this time against the Turks, lamenting, as he says, to have seen so many Christians slaughter one another. The next four years were spent in that career of fighting and adventure described in his memoirs, the account of which will not seem marvellous or extravagant when compared with other annals of that time, though sometimes in our day sneered at by closet critics as fantastical. His adventures in foreign countries were merely the experiences of a soldier learning and practicing his profession abroad, because of no occasion for its exercise at home. Nor was his career that of a Swashbuckler, as a recent biographer asserts. Men still wore armor, and the soldier's sword was not yet the almost superfluous appendage it has now become. Personal combat, such as he describes, was not unusual, and an adventurous blade like Smith could find constant use for his wits and steel.

Of the wars in which he was engaged, the history is as obscure as that of any other contest of semi-barbarians, or of the bickerings and fightings nowadays of the same regions of southeast Europe, about which we care nothing, as we read of them in the daily papers. Their history has almost no possible interest for us, except for the fact that this one man was engaged in them. What little ever was written about them— happily little—is long ago forgotten, swept into oblivion, but where it can be traced it vindicates the truth of Smith's narrative by establishing his dates and locations.

During these campaigns occurred the celebrated combat with the three Turks, effigies of whose heads appeared on Smith's crest when afterwards he found it useful to adopt a coat of arms. The story of the three Turks has been the subject of some derision on the part of incredulous critics; as also, the account of his captivity and sale into slavery, and the charming episode of that Eastern woman, with unpronouncable name, whose intercession was intended to relieve the bonds of his slavery, but, as happens in such cases, resulted in consigning him to a harsher master and more rigorous treatment. From this captivity he released himself by knocking out his master's brains and escaping on his horse.

Smith's narrative of his life and adventures at that time has been impugned as the account of a braggart and boaster. On merely literary grounds, the criticism might have some validity; for, in the direct, rough way of a man ignorant or careless of literary style, his narrative does often verge on the bombastic, with an egotism that would have been avoided by a more polished and skillful writer. That is a matter of opinion, and only mentioned as in one way touching the question of his veracity in dealing with facts. It is probable, indeed, that his narrative of those early adventures is often an understatement rather than exaggeration of facts of common experience in a life of adventure and daring. Many ot us in our day, survivors, or acquainted with the survivors, of a war, know men who tell sober truth about adventures that it would be difficult to make appear credible if written out in plain prose. It is one of the most difficult of arts to describe credibly such an experience, especially when writing so much about one's self, as Smith necessarily did. Nobody makes any claims for him as a literary artist. As he says in the preface to his History : "Where shall we look to find a Julius Cæsar whose achievements shine as clear in his own commentaries as they did in the field?"

After some ten years of this life of adventure and wandering, which, if you know how to read him, despite the rudeness of his style, may prove interesting as any romance, he returned to England in 1604, the year after Elizabeth's death. He was then twenty-five years old, with character developed and mind trained by long experience in war and association with men of all sorts and conditions, and with knowledge of lands and peoples gained by travel in most of the then known world. Young, brave, handsome, in these years of war and adventure, he had won his way from plain John Smith, private in the ranks, to the rank of captain, a title representing much higher rank than the same grade now. The title, however, carried not much weight at home among Englishmen, who knew little and cared less for any distinction or rank gained in foreign countries. John Smith was probably less well known than some other captains who joined the expedition to Virginia. Once again in England, he found that the dire threats and dangers of Spanish armadas and popish conquest were no longer objects of apprehension, and that Protestant England was eagerly discussing and preparing for the great plans and enterprises opening for Anglo-Saxon genius, now ready to try its hand, among other things, at American colonization. Such a scheme would at once naturally attract the attention and enlist the energy of a man like Smith, doubly qualified for undertaking it by the inclination which prompted him to adventure and the training that had developed qualities needed for such enterprise. Having gone through and experienced nearly all that the known world could offer, why not try his fortunes in that unknown world beyond the great waters, waiting for English hands and English minds to come and develop its boundless possibilities? Spain and Spaniards, whom Englishmen hated as Satan incarnate, had reaped there boundless wealth which had supplied means for efforts that almost conquered England. Why not compete with them for the new world and a share of its riches? Here was field for adventure and an opening for his talents. At first he made arrangements to join an expedition to South America, which failed. Disappointed in this, he joined his fortunes to those of the London Virginia Company, then planning what proved to be the first successful English effort at permanent colonization in North America.

It is unnecessary to explain the organization of the Virginia Company, more than to say that the expedition for the colony was organized on commercial lines. *It was not*, as it is sometimes assumed, a government undertaking, sent out by the Crown, but a private enterprise, organized under charter. Nor have we time to dwell on the incidents of the voyage, of which the records are scant. It was a voyage longer and greater, relatively, than one now around the world, and more uncertain than a present trip to Central Africa. Meagre as are the details of the voyage, we yet know that before it was over dissensions arose and cliques were formed, as was natural among men so situated, without recognized head or chief. For it was one of the faults of the expedition that it was sent with sealed instructions, and that the designated officers were not known till these instructions were opened after landing in Virginia. Newport, the captain of the fleet, had no official authority over the colonists, but was only the ship captain, chartered to bring them over as passengers. The officers being not yet known, there was no official head or control; no discipline but that of the captain of the ship, who, with a sailor's contempt for landsmen at sea, kept such order as he could with so motley a gang of passengers. Here were one hundred and fifty men cooped up for four months on three ships, of which the largest was smaller than the coal schooners of to-day. Nothing else, not even camp life, so develops characteristics, or makes people acquainted with each other so quickly, as an ocean voyage. They soon know, or fancy that they know, everybody and everything about everybody else on board. If such be true of passengers on a roomy ship, with every appliance for comfort, how much more so of men crowded and huddled in little vessels with scant room and with roughest of fare and accommodations. And this crowd—of such men as these were—of all sorts, from the gentlemen captains, and the captains who were not gentlemen, through all grades, down to the anonymous vagabonds classified generically as so many Dutchmen. Most of them, of course, were rough men, such as were needed for the rough work before them. It was just such a crowd as would be drummed together now for an expedition of unknown adventure and peril. Thus jumbled together, all the human nature in them was developed. Everybody got to know everybody else and to find out what was in, and, what is more, not in his neighbors and companions, with the inevitable result of little cliques and parties. In such circumstances, so shrewd an observer as John Smith, part of whose professional training and business it was to judge human character, had doubtless before long measured up and taken the calibre, physical and mental, of every man on board.

Of course, bickerings and quarrels arose, as seems inevitable when men are thus thrown together and cut off from the rest of the world. A notable instance of this, in our times, is the recent Stanley expedition, provided with every appliance and officered beforehand with picked men. Yet, read their accounts since their return, and on them try to decide which officer least deserves hanging. In these differences and disputes the personality of Smith doubtless asserted itself, and drew to him the following—clique it you choose—that will always be attached to a strong, masterful character. Long before the voyage was over, envy or jealousy, or what not, had created a combination against Smith, charging him with mutiny, and even accusing him of intent to make himself king of the new country to which they were bound. This went so far that there was some talk of hanging when they stopped on the way at one of the West India islands. Smith, however, evidently felt himself strong enough in his following to defy and treat with contempt the threatened danger, which he met in characteristic way; as, writing about it afterwards, he says: "A pair of gallows was made, but Captain Smith, for whom they were intended, could not be persuaded to use them." The combination against him was, however, strong enough to put him under arrest and keep him out of his rightful place and rank as a member of the Council after landing in Virginia.

At length, after four months' tossing on the wintry Atlantic, instead of a five or six weeks' voyage as expected on leaving England, the colonists arrived inside the Capes, astonished and delighted with the beauty of the country before their eyes. In this sylvan and watered paradise, so enchanting after their long and weary voyage, they probably expected to find a population gentle and semi-civilized, such as the Spaniards had encountered in more southern regions, among whom they could peaceably settle and establish commercial relations.

But—and mark this as a key to the whole subsequent situation—they had scarce put foot on shore when they found that they had to deal with the original Virginia Indian, contesting his native soil, who made a savage attack on them, wounding two of the party, and only driven back by the ship's cannon; an attack that proved conclusively, to anybody with sense for conclusions, that the first, most peremptory of all questions, and immediately before them, was one not commercial, but purely military, demanding a soldier's head and hand. Commercial matters must perforce be postponed. Yet, on opening their sealed orders, as required to do on making land, they found provisions for a president and thirteen councillors, and an admirable set of commercial instructions, with injunction of peace policy toward the natives, and with special directions to find a route to the South sea—as the Pacific ocean was then called—which was supposed to be but a short distance across the country. How far distant it might be they knew not— the art of reckoning longitude being yet unknown—though they knew they were in about the latitude reached some years before by Drake in the Pacific.

Under their organization Captain Wingfield was appointed President, and the designated councillors were duly sworn in, except John Smith, who was under arrest! the man of all others who, some of us think, should have been in absolute supreme command to promote the speedier settlement of the country and the earlier development of civilization in this Commonwealth. Thus a commercial and colonizing expedition found that the first thing before them was to effect a lodgement in the country in the face of a native force, of whose strength they were ignorant, but of whose hostile and determined character the first experience had given decisive example and proof. This, of course, was a purely military problem. The very place of settlement was determined by military reasons that compelled them, in selecting a site for the colony, to disobey their instructions; which were to settle on high ground as far up a river as they could go. Instead of selecting such a location they stopped at Jamestown, because its peninsula, as it then was, was more easily protected from attack, and the surrounding water afforded means of defence by ships; at Jamestown, on the verge of an almost tropical forest, and surrounded with marsh and swamp reeking with malaria and miasma; on James river low-grounds, where, after near three centuries cultivation and clearing, the unacclimated stranger is even yet not safe from chills and ague without a liberal supply of quinine and whiskey.

Though under arrest at the time of landing at Jamestown—at any rate not yet admitted to the Council, to which the instructions appointed him—Smith accompanied Newport on that first trip up the river, exploring as far as the present site of Richmond. Newport doubtless saw the value of such a man in the fighting business probably before them, and took him along, arrest or no arrest. On return from the trip up the river they learned that another proof of the character of the situation had been given the day before, when four hundred Indians surprised and assaulted the fort, and were only beaten off by the guns of the ships. This attack was a complete surprise, while the colonists were planting corn, unarmed and unguarded. In the battle one man was killed; most of the Council and thirteen others were wounded. Almost daily attacks after this but emphasized the fact that the only and essential question before them was one of self-preservation against the attacks of a determined and hostile population.

Newport sailed on his return to England June 22d, leaving one hundred and five colonists, with thirteen weeks' supply of provisions, such as they were, and the smallest of the ships that had brought them over. Before his sailing, Smith was sworn in as a member of the Council, June 10th, and it is significant that on the next day "articles and orders for gentlemen and soldiers were upon the court of guard"; that is, military discipline was established, and recognition taken of the stern facts of the situation, in face of the lurking Indians, who were only watching for any chance to attack and exterminate the colony. Soon after Newport's departure, under the growing heat of summer, the baleful effects of climate and river low-grounds and swamps, began to develop. What with insufficient and bad provisions, brackish water, and swamp malaria, the result was that in three months half of their number were dead, and the survivors were an almost helpless lot of miserable creatures, shaking with fever, ague, and dysentery. It was a frightful, almost desperate condition, in which the Indians were kept off only by dread of the white man's fire-arms. Dismal as was the prospect before the colonists, there was, besides, the ominous memory of the fate of their countrymen at Roanoke, only some twenty years before, whose dark tragedy remains to-day one of the mysteries of history. The only hope of safety seemed to be in the promised return of the ships from England.

Smith charges Wingfield, the president, with incompetence, and says he was generally hated by all, which seems probable and well established from the fact that he was soon deposed by his fellow-colonists,

Ratcliffe being elected in his stead. From the accounts that survive, it seems that all the exploring and trading with Indians for corn was done by Smith; and without derogating from or disparaging others, it seems abundantly proved that he was literally the life of the colony. Without his untiring enterprise, supported by dauntless courage, in finding and procuring supplies from the Indians, impending starvation and pestilence would have wrought their fatal effects on the colonists, or else reduced them to such helpless extremity as would render their extermination practicable and easy at the hands of the ever hostile Indians.

Such, imperfectly sketched, was the man, and such his circumstances at the end of that year of the first settlement on our shores. We come now to the matter that is our main point of interest, both for itself and as involving the question of Smith's character and veracity.

On the 10th of December, Smith started on the memorable Chickahominy trip, which was undertaken mainly for the purpose of finding and securing supplies, while also exploring and getting what knowledge he could of the utterly unknown region to which the river might lead. For this trip he took with him ten or twelve men, which was, of course, allowed by the President and Council; for it is to be remembered that at this time Smith was not President or Governor, but only a member of Council. Entering the mouth of the Chickahominy river ten or fifteen miles above Jamestown, he there left the barge, with seven men, under orders not to go ashore, but to watch for Indians. With two other men and an Indian guide he continued the ascent of the river in a canoe. Ascending as far as practicable in his boat, he went ashore, left his two companions with the boat, himself with the Indian advancing up the river bank or into the forest. Suddenly he was attacked by a band of Indians, and was captured. *Captured!* a prisoner in the hands of the original red American Indian, and not tomahawked on the spot! because, from all we know of Indian character and methods—*only* because—reserved for torture or other solemn execution. *Captured!* and not slain on the spot! but carried around for four or five weeks through different tribes and villages, and then, without ransom or exchange, voluntarily released and sent back to Jamestown *alive!* which is *the* main fact, and the most marvellous and improbable—but for its indisputable truth—in his whole career ; a fact more marvellous than any story of rescue by Pocahontas, or by any other means; and, we may say, a fact inexplicable and impossible without some such means of deliverance from Indian vengeance, whose laws are well known to us.

Of three other men captured at the same time, two were slain on the spot; the other was tortured and burned after the usual Indian fashion. I emphasize this fact of return alive, because, aside from and more than any story, true or false, of means of deliverance, it is the marvellous feature of the whole story, not questioned or disputed by anybody.

So far, including the safe return to Jamestown, the facts are undisputed. The world for generations has known the story of that rescue and deliverance; how, when Smith was taking, as he thought, his last look at this world, that Indian maid, with swift feet and beating heart, rushed amid the throng of dusky warriors, stayed the clubs upraised to beat out his brains, and at the risk of her own life saved his.

That story is told in Smith's own words, in his own authentic book, published by himself. But now come the cavils of critics, who, in denying the Pocahontas rescue, dispute a

simple, probably only possible, explanation
of the main fact, infinitely more marvellous
and improbable, and tell us that the Pocahontas story is a fiction, invented sixteen
years after the event; thereby raising the
question and making the charge that Smith
is a gasconading braggart and liar—for that
is what the cavils mean and amount to. The
charge has been so often repeated of late
years, and on such seemingly respectable
authority, that many of us have had misgiv-
ings and fears that it might prove to be well
founded, and result in waking us from a
fool's dream of heroism and devotion, with
which we had decorated our history; into
belief of which we and the generations before us had been beguiled by a braggart's
vanity. The grave seriousness, to say nothing
of the occasional sportive wit, with which
the charge was and is made, the learning by
which it is supported, seemed to justify the
apprehension that " the legend must go," as
expressed in one of the latest utterances con-
cerning it.

We may be glad to find some reasons en-
titling us to have our opinion and retain our
belief about a matter of some interest to us,
and of some value in our history.

The charge is founded on statements in

a book attributed to and bearing Smith's name, which was, we may almost say, discovered not many years ago; brought to light by the zeal that of late years has so diligently ransacked ancient records and books for everything bearing on our earlier American history. This little book, the so-called "Relation of Virginia," is the earliest known published work relating to the settlement at Jamestown, having been printed in London in 1608—the year of the captivity. Among other things, it contains a version of Smith's captivity so different from the account published some years later in his History as to cast the gravest suspicion on one of the two narratives, which are utterly inconsistent—in effect contradictory. If one is true, the other is false.

The critics insist that the account in the earlier "Relation" must be accepted as the true and credible story, because written just after the captivity, when the events were recent and fresh in mind; and charge that the story of rescue by Pocahontas as told in the History, so familiar to us and generally received, is an invention—"embellishment," they call it—prompted by vanity and by Smith's fondness for making a hero of himself. Let us look into the credibility of the

"Relation," and see what is Smith's responsibility.

There are three books on Virginia bearing Smith's name: The "Relation," published 1608; the "Map with Descriptions," &c., published 1612, and the "History of Virginia," published 1624. With only the first and the last named—the "Relation" and the "History"—we have now to do as relating to the Smith captivity, and bearing on the question of his credibility and veracity.

The so-called "Relation" is a small pamphlet, of less than forty pages, so rare and obscure, so lost in oblivion, that it may be said to have been practically unknown till unearthed and brought to light in recent years. In 1866 it was reprinted in Boston with elaborate introduction and notes by Mr. Charles Deane, a New England scholar and writer. In his notes to this edition Mr. Deane discovers the discrepancies between the narratives of the "Relation" and the "History," and grounds the charges against Smith's veracity.

This "Relation" was originally, in 1608, edited and published in London, by one J. H., whoever he was; for nobody knows. It purported to be, and probably is, a version of a letter from Virginia by Smith to a friend

in England, though the question of authorship might be contested. The unknown
editor, J. H., fortunately wrote a preface to
his publication, from which we know that,
as printed by him, it is certainly not the letter
as originally written. In this preface it is an-
nounced that, " Somewhat more was by him
the author written, which being as I thought
fit to be private, I would not adventure to
make public." The case as against Smith
might be rested just here, on the reasonable
ground that the omitted or suppressed parts
of the letter, if really his, may have been
statements that would make the narrative
entirely or substantially consistent with the
account published by him in later years, for
which he is responsible. For you cannot
hold a man responsible for statements attributed to him in a publication acknowledged
to be garbled, as against his own genuine
and authentic, but different, statement about
the same transaction; and certainly not
when the first statement or publication was
utterly unauthorized, and never acknowledged by him, as we shall see is the case
here. Unless, indeed, he is proven to be so
unreliable that his authentic statements cannot be accepted, or that they are inconsistent
with well-known facts; but we do not now

insist on this view of the case, especially as the first edition of the letter was printed without the preface referred to, published without any explanation, and without any name of author on the title-page. It must be borne in mind that the letter, if Smith's, was printed without his knowledge or consent, he being at the time in Virginia, three thousand miles away, and that the editor and publisher of it acknowledges an unauthorized and even surreptitious possession and handling of a private letter, when he says, in his preface: "Happening upon this relation by chance, as I take it, at second or third hand, I thought good to publish it."

The preface, as a whole, is a curious example of the worst style of its day, a mixture of the then fashionable conceits prevalent among euphuistic wits and witlings. From its opening sentences of poor stage-player illustrations to its closing words of affected piety and zeal for religion, it is tainted with affectations that arouse suspicion of the genuineness of the work it heralds to the world of courtly sinners and puritan saints, who might be interested, or induced to become interested, in the novel enterprise described and advocated in its pages.

So much, in brief, for the character of the

preface. As to the "Relation" itself, it begins abruptly with statements about making land and the arrival at Jamestown, nominating the Council, and electing the President; all of which is disposed of in less that twenty lines. Then follows, with some detail, an account of the exploring trip up the river as far as the present site of Richmond. With the rest of the narrative, describing the condition of things at Jamestown during that summer, and Smith's expeditions for supplies, we have not now to do, till it comes to the account of his capture by the Indians. So far the "Relation" agrees mainly with Smith's narrative in his later "History." The point of interest to us now is its version of the captivity as being so much at variance with Smith's account of that experience, published in his "History" sixteen years later. This variation in the two books is the ground of the critics' charge that the later narrative—describing the rescue by Pocahontas—is fiction and romance, invented by Smith to embellish his story and magnify his exploits. This requires some brief recital of the "Relation's" narrative.

After describing the trip up the Chickahominy river, the surprise and capture by the Indians, the "Relation" proceeds with the statement that the Indians "requited him with abundant food and kindly speeches," and that, while he momentarily expected execution, they yet "used him with all the kindness they could devise to content him and disarm his fears." It goes on to tell how they fed him every day with more venison than ten men could eat, and how "their longer acquaintance but increased their better affection;" and how he amused and entertained his captors by descriptions of everything he could make them understand about civilized ways and beliefs. It then proceeds with an account of their carrying him around through the villages, and of his reception by Powhatan, who welcomed him with kindly words and abundance of savage hospitality, assuring him of his friendship, and of release within four days. With this assurance of friendship, Powhatan invited him to forsake Jamestown and come to live with him, promising "to give me corn, venison, or what I wanted to feed us; we should make hatchets and copper for him, and none should disturb us. This request I promised to perform; and thus having, with all the kindness he could devise, sought to content me, he sent me home."

Such, substantially, is this "Relation's"

account of a white man's experience as a
prisoner in the hands of the original Virginia Indians, who had shown most determined and deadly hostility against the English from the first day of their landing on the
shore of Chesapeake bay. After the fight
and capture, there is hardly any suggestion
of mortal peril, and almost the only intima-
tion of danger and fear is when carried to
to the spot where Robinson, one of his companions, lay slain, it says: "I expected
when they would execute me"; and again
at Powhatan's village: "So fat they fed me
that I much doubted they intended to sac-
rifice me."

There is not one word about being dragged
out for execution, or about any rescue by
Pocahontas, whose name is not even mentioned. On the contrary, it is a narrative of
a pic-nic trip among friendly natives of the
country, a winter idyl of Indian life. And
what is the reason or consideration for this
exceptional, this unparalleled, clemency of
these Indians to their prisoner? Why, after
killing his captured companions, did they
spare his life and send him home to their enemies unharmed and without ransom or consideration? Why such friendly conduct to
the man whom they probably considered the

head-devil of the white-faced intruders, come to occupy their lands and drive them from their homes? To these questions, naturally arising after reading such a narrative, we seek in vain for answer.

This "Relation" gives absolutely not one word of such reason or explanation; nor does it attempt any solution of the enigma presented by its version of an unparalleled experience, but leaves the undoubted fact of Smith's returning alive involved in a mystery without any hint or suggestion of explanation.

It needs not the wisdom of editors and critics to tell us that if THIS thing be true—if this "Relation" be an authentic and credible account of Smith's release from captivity—then, necessarily, the story of the intended execution and the rescue by Pocahontas, as told in the later "History," IS mere fiction and invention.

BUT doesn't anybody who ever read a chapter of American Indian history know that this account in this "Relation" is NOT true; that it is palpably false, contradicted by all the circumstances of the case, and contradicted by all our knowledge of Indian character and methods, derived from three centuries experience with them? Just think of it! Captured red-handed in desperate fight, after slaying three of the enemy before he threw away his arms and surrendered himself; a helpless prisoner in the hands of a deadly foe, whose first law is revenge, and whose religion it is to kill his enemy; and who, disdaining as weakness any sentiment of pity or mercy, either tomahawks and scalps on the spot, or else reserves his prisoner for torture at the stake, with every device of savage cruelty. Yet we are told that the aboriginal Indian takes this prisoner, his deadly enemy, invading his country and rights, carries him on a four weeks' jaunt through his villages, gives him friendly entertainment, and sends him home unransomed and with scalp untouched; and all this without any reason or explanation assigned for such an astonishing statement. Such a falsehood carries its own refutation in its very absurdity, and is a hundred fold more incredible than any story of rescue by Pocahontas. As the narrative stands in that "Relation" it could not be believed on John Smith's own authority. But no jot of responsibility can attach to Smith for it or its publication, as will be readily shown by recital of known facts about the book.

So much for the contents of the book.

What is its history? A brief review will
show that it is as suspicious in character as
its account of that captivity is improbable
and false. There were at least three editions
of the little pamphlet. As said before, the
original editor and publisher fortunately
wrote a preface to one of the editions, in
which, among other things more or less curious and suspicious, he undertakes to explain
and apologize for matters that certainly need
explanation even more than he has given.
The three or more editions were successively
issued with three different title-pages, with
three various ascriptions of authorship. The
first—most probably the first—ascribes the
book to "A gentleman of the Colony "—no
name being given. The second title-page
ascribes it to " Thomas Watson, gentleman
of the Colony "; while in the third title it is
ascribed to " Capt. John Smith, Coronel of
the Colony." The first two editions were
issued without any preface. To the third
edition, ascribed to Smith, the skulking editor and peddler of another man's private letter—hiding his own name under initials

---

NOTE.—This title "Coronel" is suspicious, and
should discredit the book. There was no such office.
Smith was known and designated only as "Captain,"
and was only member of Council.

probably false—prints the preface, explaining and excusing, among other things, that "the chief error was that (in previous issues) "for want of knowledge of the writer some "were printed under the name of Watson, "by whose occasion he knows not, unless it "were the overrashness or mistaking of the "workmen (printers)." As if, in that day of strictly licensed presses, when the printer's ears might be the penalty for such a blunder, he would yet dare to put on the title-page a name not given him by the responsible author or editor for whom he was printing.

After this apology or explanation of the Watson name on the title-page of previous issues, the editor goes on to say that he has since learned that the said discourse, the "Relation," was written by "Captain Smith, one of the Council in Virginia," and then adds the fact that he had taken the liberty to suppress parts of the letter. On the statements of the editor himself, we might contest the question of authorship, and deny in toto any responsibility of Smith for any part of the performance. Such is the ground taken by J. Paine Collier, a high authority in English bibliography, who believes that Watson was the author of the tract. It is probable, however, that the "Relation" is mainly

Smith's letter perverted and distorted by this editor, J. H., for a purpose, of which we may fairly conjecture.

It is not incumbent on us to explain the genesis or motive of this fraudulent little pamphlet, which, as to its account of Smith's captivity, needs no further refutation than shown by its intrinsic falsehood. But, doesn't it look like a stock-jobbing trick to boom the Virginia Company's shares? Look at the time of its issue, just after the second return of the ships from Virginia without the expected gold and silver, or anything else that promised immediate profit to stockholders. Despite the Company's orders against letters bearing unfavorable news or reports from the Colony, ugly rumors were probably afloat about the hostility of the natives and the precarious state of the colonists. Unless something can be done to counteract these reports and put a better phase on the matter, the stock represents a bad speculation, and there will be small chance of inducing further emigration to a county where a man risks being scalped if he ventures outside the palisades of Jamestown. To contradict this impression, and to show that the country was not necessarily so unsafe for a white man, this unknown editor, the initialed J. H.,

takes a private letter of Smith's, or somebody else, which somehow or other had got-
ten in his hands, and by suppressions, and
perhaps some forgeries not worse than suppressions, by omission of anything suggest-
ing mortal risk or danger—by such means
as these, not yet forgotten by skillful mani-
pulators of stock markets, the clever fellow
pictures a state of things very different, we
may be sure, from the original account of
the letter itself, and represents the American
Indian as disposed to be friendly and amiable
to the foreign stranger, even when captured
in desperate fight.

Such a version, seemingly authentic, from
" a gentleman of the Colony," or, better yet,
as in the last edition, from " Capt. John
Smith, Coronel of the Colony," might easily
gain credit in England, ignorant at that time
of Indian character, where it was designed
to affect public opinion. At any rate, it
would take at least five or six months for
authentic contradiction or comment to come
from Smith, or anybody else, on the other
side of the Atlantic; while five or six weeks,
or less, was all the time needed if the scheme
proved successful, as it probably did, in keeping up the value of the Company's stock and
enabling the successful operator to unload.

The stock market had its tricks then as well as to-day, and some of the cleverest men in England were in the business. This stock-jobbing suggestion is only a theory, but it fits the case, and may do till better explanation appears. At any rate, it may explain why, having served its purpose, the "Relation" was lost in oblivion, only to reappear in our day, when rarities, however worthless intrinsically, are eagerly sought and so valued by bibliomaniacs and collectors. Deane, its modern editor, speaks of it as one of the rarest of early Americana, as it is.

To sum up the matter, this "Relation's" account of Smith's captivity is false on the face of it, contradicted by all known facts of Indian character and methods, and utterly inconsistent with all the circumstances of the case. And it is a fraud, virtually confessed in its preface, which admits suppressions— that is, garbling—of a private letter.

The critics may pin their faith to it, but they cannot fasten to Smith any responsibility for somebody else's perversions and falsehoods. He utterly ignored it when compiling his "History," in which are incorporated his own previous writings and the writings of others on Virginia. When on such authority as this "Relation" they challenge our belief and ask us to discredit Smith's authentic statement as to the incidents of that captivity, we reply in words that his great contemporary puts in the mouth of his Hamlet: "I'll take the ghost's word for a thousand pounds."

If the Pocahontas rescue is not true, then the question arises, how in the world did Smith escape death, of which no other explanation is yet offered; and next, how account for Pocahontas' frequent and familiar visits to Jamestown, and her repeated services, even at risk of her life, for the safety of the colonists, until Smith's return to England. Why the cessation of her visits after Smith's departure for England, and why a dozen other undisputed facts, easily and naturally explained by the rescue, but utterly incoherent, not to say impossible, on denial of that fact, which is the explanation and solution of so many others.

Let us turn for a moment to Smith's own account of the rescue, which supplies an explanation of his escape from death at once sufficient and natural, though extraordinary. His story of rescue is so consistent with, and explanatory of, subsequent well-known, undisputed facts, that its denial makes these facts simply unintelligible and absurd, and destroys the coherency of our early history, leaving gaps utterly inexplicable.

We followed him, in the "Relation's" account, up the Chickahominy river to the moment of his landing and capture. The narrative of the "History" proceeds with an account of the sudden surprise at the flight of Indian arrows that wounded him, and tells how he met the attack, staying the savage onset as he bound to his arm the Indian guide, using him as a shield between himself and the lurking foe; of the desperate fight, as long as fighting was possible, in which he killed three of the enemy. Wounded, and retreating with face to the foe, making his way backwards, he sank in the Chickahominy marsh; the dread of his fire-arms keeping them at bay, till near dead with the midwinter cold of that icy mud-bath, he threw away his arms and surrendered, trusting, perhaps, to hopes of mercy, but more to the wit and address that had brought him safe through so many dangers; surrendered, but expecting the next instant to feel an Indian tomahawk crashing through his brain. Think of the man's dauntless courage and marvellous address, who, when he found to his surprise that he was not to be killed on the spot, despite his scant knowledge of the

savage language, yet succeeded in beguiling
his enemy into an interest that at least de-
ferred his fate, and through the simple means
of arousing the savage curiosity, amused
them with the play of the compass needle
and such discourse as he could make them
understand. The ordinary man would at
once have given up in despair, and awaited,
with what stolid pride he could summon, the
seemingly inevitable fate, or else excited the
savage contempt by idle appeals for mercy;
but this heroic soul asserted itself when Smith
demanded to be carried to their chief, as
claiming equality with their best, and thereby
implying threat of royal revenge for harm
inflicted on such an equal.

If John Smith were the braggart, as al-
leged, he might well boast of the daring and
successful ingenuity by which he cheated the
Indian out of instant vengeance and saved
his scalp untouched; but of the arts he used,
of the cunning beguiling by which he won
mastery of their savage minds, he says little,
and his narrative is mainly occupied, not
with what he said and did, but with notices
of Indian habits and ways, and observations
on the country, and how they carried him
round from village to village, till, arriving
at Powhatan's habitation, that council was

held which delivered the sentence for which—
and only for which—his life had been spared
from the first hour of capture.

No high-wrought rhetoric could equal
Smith's description of that scene, when in
simple and graphic words he says: "But
" the conclusion was, two great stones were "
" brought before Powhatan; then as many "
" as could laid hand on him, dragged him to "
" them, and thereon laid his head, and "
" being ready with their clubs to beat out "
" his brains, Pocahontas, the King's dear- "
" est daughter, when no entreaty could pre- "
" vail, got his head in her arms, and laid "
" her own upon his to save him from death."

*And nothing else could have saved him; and
that,* and that only, is how and why John
Smith returned alive to Jamestown. A
woman's pity! Was it a savage girl's love?
We do not say, but if so, it was a love not
dishonoring to her and not dishonored by
him. She had never before seen such a
man, of Godlike power, armed with the thun-
der and lightning of heaven, as the Indians
believed, and of prowess and bearing that
more than realized the barbarian ideal of
heroism.

A clever writer of the day, whose life of
Smith is a piece of work done to order to

supply a facetious treatment of the subject, opens his first chapter with a half-sneering remark about the good fortune of a hero who links his name romantically with that of a woman. Other and baser pens have indulged in slurs against Pocahontas' good name, founding their inuendos on words used by one of the old chroniclers, which have now their ancient meaning no more than Smith's talk about the " mountains " which he found in Eastern Virginia.

We can only remark in passing that no woman's reputation has suffered from association in his writings with Smith's name. He always speaks of the women whose names occur in his works, with the loyalty and courtesy of a gentleman.

The argument of the critics, founded on the silence of the " Relation " as to the Pocahontas rescue, seems to be fortified by the fact that no contemporaneous letter or writing from the colony refers to the rescue. This looks suspicious, but a careful review of the situation at Jamestown suggests several reasons why a prudent man, who had to think for others as well as himself, should be reticent about the details of that adventure. For these reasons, it is indeed very doubtful whether on his return he told the details of that rescue, except, perhaps, to the very few in whom he could trust, and on whose discretion he could rely. Remember the well-known fact of the desperate condition of affairs at Jamestown, where demoralization was so utter that some of the leaders were planning escape on the one small ship left there by Newport; landsmen as they were, unskilled in navigation, they were willing to risk the fearful dangers of an Atlantic voyage to escape the seemingly impending fate. In such desperate straits, all discipline and control evanished, cowardice and treason assert their sway in baser natures, prompting them to embrace any means of escape for themselves. Smith knew, as well as we know now, that there were men at Jamestown who would desert to the Indians on any expectation or hope of making terms with the warriors and finding favor with Indian women. Why should he encourage any such expectation and hope by proclaiming that he owed his escape to the favor of an Indian woman? The announcement of such a fact would have encouraged the hope in would-be deserters that they might find like favor for themselves, while exchanging the miseries of what looked like a desperate situation at Jamestown for the plenty and case of the Indian villages, only ten or twelve miles away across the Peninsula. The effect of the announcement would have been tantamount to putting a premium on desertion at a time when every man was needed for defense against an Indian attack that might come any day. If this sounds like a harsh stricture against some of our first settlers, it must be remembered that there were all sorts of men in that expedition, some of them reckless adventurers, and that, in the absence of proper discipline, it looked very much like a case of every man for himself. As a matter of fact, some of them did soon after desert to the Indians, and abetted their plots against the whites.

Another reason, equally potent for silence, was the fact that the charge had been made, and was repeatedly urged, that Smith was seeking to conciliate the Indians and plotting to confirm his influence over them with a view of making himself king of the country. This accusation went so far as to charge him with intent to murder the Council as one step in furthering his ambitious designs. The zeal of factious enemies would have interpreted his rescue from death by an Indian princess as proof confirmatory of that charge, and proclaimed it as evidence of an intended alliance with the king of the country, or as opening the way for such alliance by marriage with his daughter; which charge was afterwards actually made. Why should he put into the hand of an enemy such a club to be used against himself? Or again, and more than these reasons, would the story have been credited at the time and under circumstances of such flagrant hostility as was familiar to every man at Jamestown? The marvellous fact was that Smith had escaped death. Any explanation attributing that escape to a woman's pity or favor might have been received with incredulous jeers at a braggart's romancing, unless substantiated by undoubted evidence of witnesses of the fact.

When that story was publicly told, there was and had been abundant opportunity for such evidence to support it—yea, *even from Pocahontas herself.*

We cannot here follow the history of Pocahontas, meagre as are the details known to us, but it is certain that six years after the rescue she married the Englishman John Rolfe. It is equally certain that two years later, in 1616, she was in England with her husband and child; on which occasion Smith addressed a letter to the Queen, commending

Pocahontas to Her Majesty's consideration on the ground, among other things, that she had hazarded the beating out her own brains to save his, with other instances of risking her life on behalf of the colonists.

To vindicate Smith's veracity and credibility, it is necessary to trace the publication of the story of rescue by Pocahontas. It is found that the story was published in its appropriate time and appropriate place, and could hardly have been earlier detailed in any formal announcement unless Smith meant to go out of his way to proclaim and brag about the adventure. We have seen that, as to the "Relation," with its omissions and garblings, no jot of responsibility can attach to him for that publication, for what it contains or does not contain.

His first published work is the so-called "Map and Description," issued in 1612, three years after his return from Virginia. This work is, as its title indicates, a description of the country and inhabitants, with the map, and is not a personal narrative. Next in order of publication were three books, mere pamphlets, on New England, published respectively, 1616, 1620, 1622. In one of these tracts is the first explicit statement—not a *description*—of the rescue by Pocahontas. This statement is made in a passage discussing the mode of treatment and dealing with Indians, which he illustrates by his own experience with them. The statement is made naturally and without parade, and as reference to a fact well known to everybody acquainted with the history of Virginia affairs. Its importance for us in this discussion is that it is immediately preceded by a paragraph that a man dealing in fiction—that is, lying—would never have dared to pen; for in the paragraph preceding the statement, Smith refers to four men by name, one of whom, George Percy, had been Governor in Virginia, and to others not named, to whom he appeals as witnesses and authority for his statement. It may be added that Percy was, or afterwards became, hostile to Smith, and that he, as well as others, would have been quick to denounce any statement not true of such an adventure.

The next publication, two years later, in 1624, is the "History of Virginia," which contains the narrative and details of the rescue, so familiar to us. The "History" is mainly a compilation of writings and narratives of other men, edited by Smith, his own individual contribution being comparatively but a small part of the book. Hence many of the strictures aimed against Smith are criticisms of others, whose statements he has adopted. If he took this mode of publishing in distrust of his own literary skill or ability to treat the subject at large, it yet secured the advantage of fortifying his views by the statements of other and independent witnesses. In editing and publishing under his own name he of course made himself responsible for the whole, in which he weaves together the different narratives to make a consistent and continuous history. The interest and value of the book is not in its literary style, which is rugged and uncouth, often repellant to the merely literary reader. It may be said that the book was written before style, in the modern sense, was invented. It is the unpolished utterance of a man, or rather of men, not necessarily rude themselves, giving expression to what they knew and thought of a very serious piece of work in which they had been engaged; a piece of work of transcendent interest and importance, as we now know—namely, the founding of this Commonwealth of Virginia.

The first comment on the "History" to be made in this connection is to repeat, that if it had dealt in fiction—that is, lied—about this matter of the rescue, there were plenty of

men then living in England who knew as to
its truth or falsity. Of these men, some had
been in Virginia with Smith, or after him ;
others had known and conversed with Pocahontas in England. And of them some
were his enemies, willing and eager enough
to discredit him by denouncing any fictitious
embellishments about that or any other
matter in his book. An invention such
as the Pocahontas story might have been
risked in an obscure book, not liable to criticism and hostile scrutiny; but Smith's "History of Virginia" was never obscure. From
the first day of publication, it has been an
illustrious book, whether from interest in its
subject or in its author. It was brought out
under auspices that at once gave it fame, and
made its author's reputation a thing talked
of by all men, and criticized by enemies,
when criticism was possible. It was published at the very zenith of the most splendid
development of English literature, when
Shakspeare had been dead only eight years,
and Ben Jonson was yet at the head of English letters and criticism. It was written under the auspices of, and dedicated to, one of
the most brilliant and celebrated women of
her day, at a time when dedications were

significant, implying consent and patronage in the true sense of that word.

It would be curious to know the history of Smith's acquaintance with this Duchess of Richmond, his patroness; this superb woman, whose ambition soared so high that she is said to have set her cap for the King himself. Her husband had held high position in James' court, and she had doubtless known Pocahontas on the occasion of her visit to London and presentation at court. It is not improbable that her interest in Smith was first excited by hearing from Pocahontas herself the story of the rescue. However that may be, it was through the influence of the Duchess, and at her request, that Smith compiled his "History," and to her he dedicated it in a preface that is a masterpiece of courtesy and compliment, that must have touched the pride of even so proud a woman as she.

Of course she knew all about the incidents of Pocahontas' visit to England and presentation to the Queen, only eight years before; of course, as being familiar with the court, she knew about Smith's letter bespeaking the Queen's consideration for Pocahontas on the ground of having saved his life, of which mention has been made. And yet we are asked to believe that Smith not only invented the story of the rescue, but had the daring impudence to bolster up that story by forging and printing in his "History" a purported letter to the Queen; not only that, but also had the reckless folly to refer explicitly to the rescue in a preface dedicating his book to the cleverest and most powerful woman in England, who most probably had personal information from Pocahontas herself about the incidents of Smith's experience in Virginia. The Duchess of Richmond would have made her lackies cudgel any man who would dare to put in a book dedicated to her, fantastic lies about an Indian princess whom she had probably known.

As already said, there were plenty of men, then living, willing enough to discredit Smith on this or any other matter, if such stricture were possible. Of these would-be critics, some were members of the London Company, men of wealth and position, upon whom the comments of the book tended to throw contempt, while sometimes excusing their blunders on the half-pitying ground of ignorance. These men, embittered by heavy losses in their Virginia enterprise, would have been prompted by the average human nature to vindicate their consistency. For fifteen years they had discredited Smith, rejecting all his plans and offers, and refusing him employment in their Virginia enterprise. The publication of his book, with its strictures on their policies and plans, did not, we may be sure, lessen their feeling against its author—this upstart captain, as they probably regarded him, with his title and dubious coat of arms from some half-barbarous prince of Southeastern Europe. They had kicked him out of their service, but he had ingratiated himself into the favor of the proudest woman in England and her associates, and now, under such splendid auspices, he showed the world his side of the question, illustrated and emphasized by the fact that their policy had resulted in utter and ruinous bankruptcy. With the enmity natural under such circumstances, they would have been quick to denounce the author for any manufactured item about the most striking incident of the whole book. The exposure of any such falsehood as the Pocahontas rescue—and most certainly it would have been exposed, if false—would at once have overwhelmed book and author with merited contempt.

Contrast the history of this book with that

of the so-called "Relation," on which the
modern criticism bases its attacks on Smith's
veracity; which, after serving its purpose,
whatever that was, passed into such dusty
oblivion. The "History" has always ranked
among the first and highest authorities on its
subject. Its statements of matters of fact
have never been successfully combated, and
on points of controversy its author has been
vindicated by the experience of succeeding
generations, who found the wisdom of adopt-
ing policies substantially in conformity with
his plans and ideas.

And now, having stated the character of
the "History," and indicated Smith's stand-
ing and relations at the time of its publication, when his work was, if not a refutation then certainly a challenge to his enemies and critics, we may cite a brief passage from its closing words, in which he
refers to that relation with contempt that
must have made some galled jade wince. In
describing the "Relation," it was said that
Smith utterly ignored it when compiling his
"History." But on the last page of his
work he refers to it and his critics in such
words as these:

"Thus far have I travelled in this wilder-"
"ness of Virginia, not being ignorant that"

"for all my pains this discourse will be"
"wrested, tossed, and turned as many ways"
"as there are leaves; that I have writ too"
"much of some, too little of others, and"
"many such objections. To such I must"
"answer—if any have concealed their"
"approved experiences from my knowl-"
"edge—they must excuse me. As for"
"every fatherless or stolen relation"—wasn't
it fatherless, and doesn't its initialed editor, J. H., admit in his preface that it was
practically stolen?—"as for every father-"
"less or stolen relation, or whole volumes"
"of sophisticated rehearsals, I leave them"
"to the charge of them that desire them."
"I thank God I never undertook anything"
"yet wherein any could tax me with care-"
"lessness or dishonesty, and what is he to"
"whom I am troublesome or indebted?"

Verily, as old Dibden says of him, "Smith
was the very dragon of his breed. *Nil actum
credens, si quid superesset agendum*," which is
the Latin way of saying he never thought a
job done until it was finished.

It may be said that no book stuffed with
bragging and lies could have such long and
illustrious esteem as has been given to
Smith's "History," or could have been im-
posed without detection on his own and

subsequent generations. In Virginia, Smith's "History" has been standard reading for two hundred and fifty years, acknowledged and practically unquestioned, unless by some in these later days. We may be a simple and uncritical folk, but when our belief and judgment as to a historical character are challenged, and we are told that our admiration has been wasted on a charlatan, whose boasting has deceived us, then may we raise a question as to the amount of wisdom behind the critic's utterance, and oppose to his opinion the judgment of men acknowledged as authority on any matter of history or character to which their minds have been turned. We could cite such judgments about Smith by the score, but will be content with only two, those of Mr. Jefferson and Judge Marshall. As unlike Smith in disposition and habits of life as a man could be, yet so critical a scholar as Mr. Jefferson wrote of him that "to his efforts principally may be ascribed the support of the colony against the opposition of the natives; that he was *honest*, sensible, and well-informed, though his style is barbarous and uncouth." And Judge Marshall, in his "History of the Colonies," adopts without question Smith's narrative of the Pocahontas rescue, and speaks of him in language that shows his admiration for his "judgment, courage, and presence of mind," with highest appreciation of his talents and character.

It does seem preposterous that a literary and personal charlatan could deceive the judgment of Jefferson and Marshall, and remain to be detected by the criticisms of the Deanes, Neills, Adams, and Warners. Criticism! we need and welcome criticism, intelligently applied to our early history, based on a solid foundation of truth and facts, and enlightened with some insight into human nature. But much of this criticism of Smith is of the school that denounces Christopher Columbus as a piratical knave who blundered into the discovery of America; and one of whose latest utterances is that George Washington "was an illiterate Virginia colonel, who spelt worse than a common soldier."

And yet they tell us, "the legend must go"; but when it goes—if you will pardon the quotation of the Professor's slang—it will be time for this people to be gone; to be driven from this fair portion of God's earth, made sacred by that brave man's heroism, and by the gentle pity of that Indian maid, savage though she was.

This lecture has been confined to an inquiry as to the truth of the Pocahontas rescue, wanting time for more than reference to, and brief touches on, such other points as seemed necessary for the discussion. In examining the charge of the critics against Smith's veracity, founded on the variation between the earlier "Relation" and his own account in his "History," the proof seems conclusive against the authority of that fatherless pamphlet, as any ground whereon to impeach the truth of the later and authentic narrative of his "History."

What has been said in vindication of his truthfulness may also suggest the character of the man as shown in his deeds. However we may judge these deeds, or the man generally, yet our common experience and the testimony of history is to the effect that men like Smith do not lie. They may have a streak of vanity, or what looks like it, and may be so headstrong in convictions as to incur the charge of being conceited, but they do not lie.

The captivity and rescue were in the winter of 1607–'08. We cannot now recite the history of Smith's subsequent life in Virginia, but must note that most remarkable feat of surveying ever done on this continent, the survey of Chesapeake bay and the map of the country. This work was accomplished in an open boat, with rude instruments, and with a half mutinous crew grumbling at the exposure and hardships of the trip. In spite of all disadvantages, Smith made a map that is a marvel of skill and accuracy, and the foundation of all Virginia cartography.

His life in Virginia covered a period of only two and a half years, his stay here being terminated by severe wounding from an accidental explosion of gunpowder, which compelled him to return to England for medical treatment. There is some report of his being sent home to answer charges preferred against him. What they were, if any, we do not know; but there were doubtless complaints against a man who had not much patience with idleness and vice, and who could be very disagreeble to sluggards and cowards in forcing them to take their share of labor and danger which he did not shirk himself. Short as was his stay here, is there another example of a like influence being stamped in such brief period on the history of a great commonwealth?

Elected Governor in 1608, his skill and energy were employed in putting the affairs of the colony on as good footing as practicable under difficult circumstances, and attempting to realize the expectations and demands of the home Company; which being impossible of attainment, as Smith well knew, he was persistent in urging on them a policy which kept him in controversy with, and opposition to, the London patrons. On behalf of the London Company, we must remember that they had sent the colony as a commercial enterprise, and, as business men, they were disappointed and disgusted that no return for their venture was visible; but what chance was there for profitable trade with savage Indians? And we know now that no gold is to be found in Tidewater Virginia, and that the South sea, or Pacific ocean, one object of the expedition, is three thousand miles overland from Jamestown. This stricture on the unreasonable demands of the Company, as we now know them to have been, represents very nearly the views and idea of the situation taken by Smith at the time. In response to their complaints about the poor prospect before them, coupled with threats to leave the colonists to themselves unless the next ship brought gold or news of the route to the South sea, Smith sent a letter creditable to his wisdom and manly independence, but at

the same time evidence of how lacking such
a character may be in mere worldly sense
and policy. Think of a company's agent—
for such only was the President or Governor—writing to his official board in language
that criticises their plans, and the expectations founded on them, as foolish and delu-
sive, ridicules some of their schemes, and
asks them to send thirty carpenters, black-
smiths, and such workmen, rather than a
thousand of such as had been sent, and con-
cludes by telling them that they cannot yet
look for any profitable returns.

It is small wonder that such a president,
or agent, was involved in controversy, and
that his employers in England failed to ap-
preciate a wisdom that was a reflection on,
and contradiction of, their ideas of management. Controversy! Yes, the man's life
was a controversy for the next twenty years
that has sometimes brought on him the re
proach of having quarrelled with everybody.
But we think it could be shown that it was
the controversy of a man who saw and knew
and urged the right thing to be done, and
whose every word of controversy was not
only a protest against fatal and costly errors
of judgment, but also that it carried and
urged advice, which, if followed, might have

saved the London Company from the utter bankruptcy in which it collapsed in less than twenty years. His was the controversy of the man with some foresight of the vast future possibilities of what we are now proud to call American civilization, whose history had no chance to begin till methods were adopted in consonance with what Smith had advised and urged. "Pardon me," he writes after the massacre in 1622, "pardon me, though it passionate me beyond the bounds of modesty to have been sufficiently able to foresee these miseries and had neither power nor means to prevent it." (A. 770).

But what could one man, unskilled in arts of controversy, whose soldier nature disdained cunning and devious ways of policy; what could one man, without fortune or extraneous influence, do as against the views and designs of a board of managers three thousand miles away, armed though he was with the knowledge and experience essential for the successful prosecution of the enterprise in hand. What has ever accomplished anything against British obstinacy and fatuousness in American affairs, unless it were a Nathaniel Bacon, some fifty years after Smith, with an armed colony at his back, or

George Washington, a century after Bacon, at the head of a Revolutionary army.

To state very briefly Smith's side of the controversy, the policy proposed by him looked, in the first place, to control of the Indians, whose subjugation was the first requisite for peaceful living in the country. If white men were to live here at all, there was choice of only two alternatives; either to assimilate with and civilize the natives, or to conquer and control them. Englishmen might try to civilize Indians, but they never would assimilate, nor could they make Indians assimilate with them; hence the only practical plan, as proved by all subsequent history, was to conquer and control them. But the colonists found themselves restrained and hampered from the first by the London Company's orders for a peace policy toward the natives. However well intended, all experience has shown that such policy is utterly futile; for it takes two parties to keep peace, and the American Indian has never yet reconciled himself to it on his side. The later establishment of Rangers on our frontiers, and the subsequent establishment and use of the United States army, whose almost sole reason for existence has been to control

Indians, were but the adoption of plans and policy urged from the first by Smith. After the neglect of his advice had been exemplified and its penalty so fearfully paid by the massacre of 1622, he again renewed the offers repeatedly urged before. He proposed that the London Company should give him a hundred soldiers and thirty sailors, with whom he would force the savages to leave the country or bring them into such fear and subjection as to ensure peace and security for the settlers. These soldiers he would employ in ranging the country and controlling the savages, while he would establish forts and garrisons, ready always for defense of the country, and as posts of military instruction for the colonists; which plan is almost exactly the Indian policy subsequently adopted by these United States, and the only one that has ever been effective in dealing with savages. Fearing that it might entail more than the small expense necessary in Smith's judgment, the offer was declined; and so matters drifted on till the trouble again became acute in Bacon's time, who is dubbed the Rebel for daring to take arms and incite his fellow-colonists to band themselves for self-defense against the common danger; and so on through generations, until the protests against the narrow views of boards and parliaments three thousand miles away, culminated in a Revolutionary war and these independent United States; which result was but the logical outcome, after long course of time, of the protest and controversy first stated and urged by this plain soldier, Captain John Smith.

Again—gold, silver, and a route to the South sea, were the reiterated demands of the Company. We must remember that this was in the early seventeenth century, when English colonization was in its infancy. There was no previous experience to guide them; no precedents but what they knew of Spanish conquests and settlements, which had yielded immense treasures of gold and silver to that country; while the Pacific, or South sea, had opened to them the route to the boundless wealth of the Indies. Therefore it was not an unnatural expectation of the Company in England that some such success should crown this expedition to Virginia, of which country they were more ignorant than we now are of Central Africa. Their disappointment vented itself in criticisms and complaints of the management here, and so exasperated were they at the failure to realize their expectations, that, as in the letter referred to awhile ago, they threatened to leave the colonists to their fate unless the next ships brought gold or news of the route to the South sea. We have seen how Smith answered that letter, but we cannot now go into the grounds and reasons of his telling the Company that they could not yet expect returns for their investment; nor state his arguments against this futile and insane thirst for gold. It must suffice now to say that the controversy was warm and protracted, and that after Smith's return to England the Company refused him further employment.

The verdict of history has been pronounced on the results of that controversy, and the defenders of Captain John Smith think that the verdict has vindicated him and his policy. In twenty years the Company had gone into bankruptcy, and its charter was annulled.

Was Smith a great man? Or rather, what is the measure of his greatness? As the world generally answers that question according to the degree of success achieved in life, it might be said that his life was not a success, inasmuch as he failed to achieve the objects for which he was striving. Compelled by the accident of a wound to leave Virginia, after a stay of two and a half years, he never returned, but spent the best days of his life in seemingly futile efforts to impress on others his plans and convictions as to the policy requisite for prosperity in this and other colonies. This want of success was probably due to a lack of personal address and politic art in dealing with men whose modes of thought and ways of looking at the question at issue were very different from those of a man of his training and habits of mind. Probably the very qualities that made him pre-eminent as a leader of men in emergencies demanding prompt and resolute action, unfitted him for the *rôle* of the advocate and pleader which was needed to convince the London merchants and patrons of the futility of their management, and to persuade them of the wisdom of his views, founded as these views were, on practical knowledge of the situation, derived from his personal experience. At any rate, he failed to convince them or to find means to carry out his plans. This failure must have brought him days and years of the bitterness of disappointed hopes and plans, of which, however, but little is reflected in his books.

But, despite the fact of his brief stay here, and despite the seeming failure of his after life, how almost marvellous is the influence

of his name and fame, and how it has sur-
vived and permeated Virginia and American
history. And this fame cannot be said to
be literary, for few men read Smith's "History"; but it has established itself as a tradi-
tion in the popular mind more lasting and
potent than any written page or printed
book.

What is the secret of this supremacy, and
the homage paid his memory through all
these generations? It may be questioned
whether it is due only to the hero of the adventure through which his name is most
familiarly known. Is it not also an uncon-
scious tribute to the man who first sounded
the keynote of Virginia history, to which it
has remained true in all subsequent chapters?
Virginia history is almost written in the lives
of five or six men, whose life-periods nearly
lap; and the keynote of this history is the
protest against "*prerogative*," and the assertion of the rights of self-government. The
lives of Washington and Lee, the last of our
great protagonists, embody the struggles of a
mature and well-organized commonwealth
in defense of the principles and rights asserted
in the infant state of the same community
by Smith and Bacon. For though not formu-
lated as in later times, when the mature con-

sciousness of a well-developed community could express itself, and stamp upon the page of history the definite assertion of their rights, yet the inspiration and motive of Smith and Bacon were essentially the same as those of their later and logical successors. Their earlier deeds laid the foundation on which later generations builded; their assertions of rights marked the path and blazed the way along which our subsequent history has moved.

This fact makes the consistency and essential unity of Virginia history, and has kept the character of Virginia civilization much the same through all chances and changes; and perhaps it explains the lasting interest in, and pervasive influence of, the first of our great heroes, and gives to JOHN SMITH the honored title of FATHER OF VIRGINIA.

www.ingramcontent.com/pod-product-compliance
Lightning Source LLC
Chambersburg PA
CBHW020551130626
46552CB00007B/2855

*9 7 8 1 6 3 3 9 1 2 3 9 7 *